An Analytical Contrast
of
Black and White People

Latoya S. Williams

Trock Publishing—Hanover TWP, PA
ISBN: 979-8-218-05923-1
Library of Congress Control Number: 2022915628
Title: An Analytical Contrast of Black and White People
Author: Latoya S. Williams
Digital distribution | 2022
Paperback | 2022

Dedication

A special thanks to my interviewees for your honest and much needed response. I appreciate each and every one of you.

To my wonderful children, Chakoya, Amaya, and Le'Kayla. I love you guys beyond words. If you take nothing from this, just know you can be whatever and whomever you want to be. I will forever be proud of you girls. The skies the limit, so reach for it!!!

Mommy Loves you!

Quote: Declaration of Independence

All individuals are created equal
—Thomas Jefferson

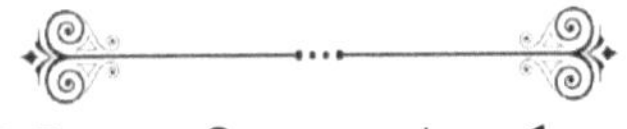

Note from Author

This book was not intended to offend anybody but just a reality that things are always Black and White. I know that's part of a saying, "everything is not always Black and White," but in this case it is. The inequalities that we as humans face every day is soaring. This is mainly because of the differences in ethnicities. There is always going to be a fine line between the injustices that separate Black and white people. It doesn't always have to be political. Our everyday lives account for how different we really are. This makes up humanity for the human race.

Thank you.

Prologue

We would all like to believe that we are all the same. I hear people say all the time, I don't see color, we're all the same." How we would love for that to be true, but it's not. There have been plenty of people that write about the difference between black and white people. How we are offered different things because of the color of our skin, how we are treated different because of the color of our skin. But, nobody really talks about how different we love, how different we eat, how different we dress, how different we do our hair.

I'm going to analyze the many different reasons why Black and White people are all different, and make you understand that Black and White people are not the same. We are all human beings, but our way of life and intentions are all different.

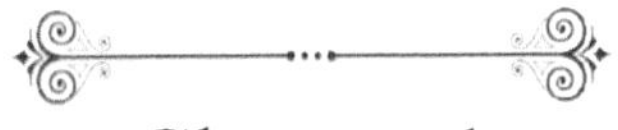

Chapter 1
The Beginning

Black and White people were never treated as equals. White people always had a better chance at life, careers, and raising children. Black people have always been prohibited to do these things. Even though it happens and makes history, it is still a forbidden gesture to White people. Don't get me wrong, all White people don't act like that, but racism still exists and will until the end of time. I don't know if it is worst now or back then.

According to our history, the inequality started back in slavery. African Americans were from Africa. Africans were forced to work in the New World. They had limited rights, and they were denied the ability and equality to share in the economic, social, and political progress of the United States. Nevertheless, African Americans have made many contributions to American history and culture (Lynch). There may be some discrepancies on how much rights African American people actually had but according to an article by Henry Drewry with Scholastic.Com, in 1857 the Dred Scott v. Sanford case of the Supreme Court placed the authority of the Constitution behind decisions regarding the treatment of Blacks(Drewry). Now according to the Dred Scott decision, even if you were a free African American, you were not intended to be included as a " citizen" in the Declaration of Independence, and therefore could not claim any of the rights and privileges that were stated in that document (Drewry). That is some interesting information that would undermine certain articles or pieces of history that says otherwise.

Black ancestors came to America as slaves and not as willing immigrants. They were promised "life," liberty and the pursuit of happiness" as stated in the Declaration of Independence. These rights were selfishly ignored by the original constitution (CRF).

Though they made many contributions to the United States, Black Americans were victims of slavery. The struggle for freedom and equality had just begun (Constitutional Rights Foundation). Our nation's founders owned slaves. George Washington, our first president was one of the largest slave owners. There were some others (CRF). This piece of history allows us to understand and question the points being made in this literature. Life was already categorized for us.

The Abolishment of Slavery on December 18, 1865, which was adopted from the 13th Amendment officially freed the Black people (History.com). On September 22, 1862, Lincoln issued a pre-emancipation proclamation, which stated that as of January 1, 1863 "all enslaved people in the states currently engaged in rebellion against the Union, shall be free" (Lincoln). He didn't free all the slaves until the 13th amendment as discussed earlier.

The end of slavery did not bring equality for Black Americans. Southern states started passing their own laws to overpower black people (CRF). This created

more segregation for Black and White people, which
led to the denial of rights discussed in the next
chapter.

Chapter 2
Rights

Black and White people do not possess the same rights. Rights are defined as "a moral or legal entitlement to have or obtain something or to act in a certain way" (dictionary.com). Which is just one of the meanings of "Rights." In this case the meaning fits the situation. This country has a lot of work to do as far as equal rights for Black and White people. Black people constantly struggle with the inequalities that are set forth for their race. There is no secret that Black people are treated unfairly than White people. This has been an issue and concern for decades. There has been research and surveys that compare percentages pertaining to certain categories that show how Black and White people are categorized by advantages or disadvantages.

Too bad we're not going to get into all of that. The purpose is to give you the differences from an actual human perspective, minus the percentages given by a national database. Although it may be accurate, it is sometimes better to hear it by mouth from numerous people that it actually affects, rather than people that have no idea. Anyway, back to the facts and conversation of "Rights."

Without sounding so political and stuff. The 14th Amendment, which was set into the Constitution in 1868, gave Black people equal protection under the law. In 1870, the 15th Amendment gave Black people the right to vote. But in Southern states back then there were what they called "Jim Crow" law. In some states they still practice these laws. The "Jim Crow" laws were set in place to remove Black people from civilization.

Black people couldn't use the same public facilities as White people. They couldn't live in the same towns or kids go to the same schools. Interracial marriages were illegal, and most Black people couldn't vote because they couldn't pass the literacy tests (History.com).

Thus, in the Northern states, "Jim Crow" laws weren't practiced. Black people were still discriminated against. They were discriminated against at the workplace, when trying to buy a house or even get an education.

Just to give you a little bit of history, not until Black people threatened to march on Washington to demand equal employment rights, did President Franklin D. Roosevelt issue an Executive order on June 25, 1941. This order opened up national defense and government jobs to all Americans regardless of race, color, or national origin (History.com).

At the time there was segregation. Which was the separation of Black and White people. It divided us in so many disturbing ways. Black people had to sit in the back of buses, while White people were able to sit in the front. This would lead to the Civil Rights Movement that Dr. Martin Luther King Jr., would lead as a part of his role as a prime minister. The organization was called the Montgomery Improvement Association (MIA). It was formed to fight for Civil Rights (History.com)

The Civil Rights Movement was a time of

empowerment. Its efforts brought about legislation to end segregation. It also brought to abolish discrimination against employment and housing practices (History.com). This was a new move for Black people. This was a breakthrough for all mankind, whether you accepted it or not. It made history. Black America was moving in the right direction, with some obstacles still to come. Rights for White people were very different.

White people had all the privileges. They ruled the country. It is still true to date. They have a lot of power. They sit amongst congress and make laws. Being white gives you certain advantages that Black people just don't have. That's a big difference between Black and White people.

Just to touch on a few things without sounding like a spokesperson for a magazine. Racial preferences have had a long history in this country (RACE). In the earlier days around like the 17th century, the Europeans replaced the African slaves. They were then awarded new rights, entitlements, and great opportunities. The Europeans were White. They were given first dibs on the U.S Army, they were able to become citizens. At that time, only citizens could vote, own property and be in office (RACE).

White people had all the federal programs catered to them. The Government designed a program for mortgage seekers based on race. But the only race getting approved for a home loan was White people. The Government gave out millions of dollars. In that era, they called it "White Privilege." Not so nicely put (haha). It represented the freedom of choices in life that White people had. "White people were so privileged they didn't even think it was racist" (Starkey). And again, when I say "Rights," I mean just that. White people had the right to do things that Black people dreamed of.

Times have definitely changed, but it's far from fixed. Just a look back, at the beginning, when a lot of us were not around. The history that you research and read about, how a lot of things came about. The reasons why there is a Black and White. A little bit of History can go a long way. I just wanted to give you guys a little information that I learned while doing some research. Again, If I say this a lot, it's not meant to offend anybody. This information if not known already gives you a bit of a background on why today Black and White people have such a division, where it's hard to integrate as a whole. It started so long ago that it will take an eternity to fix. If we have that long (haha). Okay, since we broke the ice a little bit, let's talk about the fun stuff (yayyyyyyy) (haha).

The next chapters will focus on real differences as far as life goes. What makes us different as a human being in our society today. Topics that nobody talks about outside of friends and family. Everything is always so political these days. Well NOT HERE! We are going to talk about our home lives. How we live on a day to day basis. We'll conduct some interviews to get different perspectives from both parties. So, shall we begin, I hope you enjoy.

Chapter 3
Love

Everybody should love the same, but that is not always the case. We all love different. Because the world is always being categorized by Black and White, we do not love the same things. White people love their animals. They think of them as family. They think their animals are their children. I am nowhere near prejudice, because I love all people, I just dislike a lot of people (haha). I will just never understand how an animal gets so much attention and privileges. Some White people really go too far. Like walking their dog or cat around in a damn baby stroller. Letting them sleep in their beds. Feeding them human food all the time. They are supposed to eat animal food. They kiss their pets in the mouth and shit. (ugghh). Make you wanna throw up. I get the love, but some things should not be done. That's just nasty. Be mad at me later. (haha). Those same animals kill you later. There have been so many animal incidents with their owners. You can't trust them. They are wild animals, not your flesh and blood (cthu). Me and my kids have had plenty of animals, but we are just not animal people. Although my two oldest daughters said they are getting dogs when they get a place together, isn't that nice (haha), I love them. I think they said a Husky and a German Shepherd for protection. I actually asked my wonderful middle child about what kind of dogs her and her sister were getting and she says, we are getting a great big Husky and a great big German Shepherd, I don't care what Koya wants" (smh).

My Maya, she is the worst, but I love her though (haha). She is a hot mess (lol). My kids don't want to do anything for the animal, but they want an animal. So it seems that I am actually allergic to dogs, cats, (which I hate) and dander. I am not an animal fanatic, but I do like some animals. They are very interesting species. The crazy part is everybody's dogs seem to like me. I don't know why. Not only do I have a way with people, I have a way with animals too (lol).

White people really go all out for their pets. It's a beautiful thing, but I just think sometimes they really do weird stuff to and for their pets. They go overboard. The craziest thing that I know of White people is when they leave their entire estate to their dog or cat (haha). I will leave it at that. Love is Love, that's the topic (lol).

On the other hand, and I say this with the utmost respect being a Black person and woman. Black people don't know how to love and take care of a pet properly. It's not alright, but our demeanor is very different (lol).

Don't get me wrong, Black people get dogs and cats, etc. But they are not sleeping in our bed, and we damn sure ain't feeding them our food that we worked hard to buy, nor will we waste our food stamps (lmao). It's the truth. We get these aggressive dogs too, pit bulls and bully's and stuff. Animals that will bite the shit out of somebody (lol). But seriously, we love different things. Like for instance, Black people get cats to catch freaking mice. We don't necessarily like them, especially since they shed so much hair. There is a reason and a purpose. White people Love cats as pets and companions. They will have 40 cats in one damn living space, like (wth), call the authorities. You see and hear this all the time on the news how some crazy cat lady has a bunch of cats all over her property, and her neighbors are sick of it. Nobody but a White lady. It's about time someone said something. That is nasty on so many levels. How do you let it get that way. I could see if you were rescuing them and try to get them a good home, but to have that many cats at a time is just disgusting, because then your home is smelly, like piss. Cat hair all over the place, litter boxes all over the house, like clean up. Everywhere you sit a cat jumps all over you. Black people don't have that problem. The fact that animals have so much maintenance (smh).

White people Love to do dangerous things for an activity or hobby, like bungy jumping and sky diving. A Black person is not dying for the cause (lol). We don't want to jump out of something we love to do. Black people love to party, we love to dance and have reunions. We love to drink and smoke. Those are some of our Loves. Not killing ourselves instantly (lol).

White people Love to diet. They are very conscious about their weight. They could weigh 100lbs and say that they need to lose weight. I don't think they realize that being that small doesn't always constitute as healthy. You need meat on your bones.

Black people on the other hand, Love to eat. We want to look good and weigh a decent amount of pounds, but we Love food too much and we don't want to do the things that we should be doing to lose the weight. A diet is like a sin for a Black person. You'll get somebody to say things like "girl you look good, you don't need to lose no weight," girl bye, meanwhile you're fat as shit (lmao). Your legs are rubbing together, you can't breathe, and you don't even have asthma (lol). Black people love to eat. Black people love to cook. We cook wholesome foods like soul food, is what it's called. Collard Greens, baked mac and cheese, pork, chicken and ribs and shit. That's what you call a meal. We love to get busy in the kitchen.

White people love to cook but their cooking and what they eat, is a little different. They love to cook pastas and pizza. They love to eat salads and foods you never heard of unless you went on a damn cooking show (lol). More about foods and what we eat in the next chapter. White people love to hate Black people. Not all but some. They love to hate us because they think that we have bombarded their country. Which clearly is not the case. White people love to make it seem like we did something to them.

Black people love to see people getting along. They love to see other Black people win. They love to see other Black people be successful and open Black-owned businesses. Don't get me wrong, not all Black people have that in them. People do tend to get jealous, but it is realized that we have the potential to be just as great as White people.

We (Black and White people) have, the ability to love beyond limits, but society sometimes interferes with what should be, rather than what is. Love is love and can be felt by all. Love one another, because at the end of the day, we as Americans are all we got. If we don't love each other for who we are, we could never stand united as one.

Chapter 4
Food

When we talk about food, we talk about how it's prepared, who actually cooks the food and lastly, what we actually eat. I know that from being a Black woman myself, I was taught how to cook at a very young age. I was raised in Brooklyn, NY, which is the big city. I do know that city life and suburban life is very different on how food is done and what is being cooked. In the suburban areas, there are a lot of different cultures. There are Polish people, Black people, White people, Muslim people. In the big cities, you get mostly Black people, a sprinkle of White people and some others. You are going to get a mixture of them all. In the Developments (project areas) where I was raised, the food is amazing. New York has amazing places to eat, and you can get anything you want from NY. Some places are slow in getting certain foods or they just never heard of it. Like I live in Pennsylvania all of my adult life, except for a move to New Jersey for a year. There are a lot of foods that these stores out here never heard of. I had to travel outside of here to the city to buy certain foods, like real pastrami, pudding, sage sausage, just to name a few. The pudding and sage sausage are Southern foods. My nanny was from down South, so the pudding, sage sausage, pig feet and chicken feet were dishes that I got from her. One of my favorites is dirty rice. It's sooo good (licking lips). My nana taught me a lot about foods. She made a lot of things by scratch. Like her German Chocolate cake, (hmmm). I don't like coconut, but I love mee some German Chocolate cake. She would melt chocolate bars for the actual cake part. She made her own frosting also. So, as you can see food, is a very important part of our lives. It gives us the protein and nutrients that we as humans need to survive.

In this chapter I have conducted some interviews from two white individuals and two black individuals. The purpose was to gain some human insight on what foods they were, they were brought up on, and how it was prepared, and how they incorporate their adult lives with their families. Black and White people cook and eat soo different. Being in my forties, I have tasted foods from both ethnic groups, being Black and all you can just imagine. I have eaten from all kinds of ethnic groups, but I tell you, some White people cannot cook. They don't season their damn food. It's like their scared to put some stank on it(lol).

My mother watches these cooking show and all the White people use the same seasonings, salt and pepper(smh). Like there are more seasonings than that. Where is the flavor. Where's the pazzaz. I have White friends, and I must say, some of their foods is not half bad, and they know I liked it if I gave them a compliment. I don't eat everybody's food, I am very cautious, and I like what I like. Me as a cook, because I learned from the best, I can cook pretty much anything. I never taste my food while I am cooking. I know it's weird, but I have just never done it. When the food is done, then I eat(lol). I know, I know how to cook, because I used to sell food, and my extended family of friends remind me of how good I cook, because they still want me to open that restaurant, which I am not because being a chef is not my passion. I got my business degree so that I could open up a successful soul food restaurant, but my focus is on other things. Food is just something that I can do because I can cook my ass off, and I know it's the bomb(lol).

Anyway, I don't know who taught some of these White people how to cook, but they need lessons from Black people. They are missing out on some good shit. I can pretty much probably like most people look at somebody's food and know that it's nasty. If it does not look good, I'm not eating it. I also have a habit of smelling my food, which I get yelled at by my other half and a dirty look, he hates when I do that(lol). I don't care, I have to speculate the food first(haha).

Food is also a foundation forget togethers, family reunions, parties, weddings, anniversaries, etc. All of these events require food to be successful. The difference between Black and White people is that Black people ain't coming to your house or any of the events listed above if there is no food being served, I tell you we are a total mess(haha). The first question we are going to ask is who's cooking and what are they cooking. If you don't have the right answer for a Black person, believe me when I tell you, they won't be there(haha). As soon as you hang up from a Black person after telling them about whatever you're having, and then you tell them there's no food or something crazy about the menu, better believe they're going to have some nice choice words for yo ass(lol). Ex.(ring ring)(calling cousin Shonda). Hey cousin Shonda, it's Toya, how are you? Hey, I'm calling to invite you to a little get together I'm having at my house (you give them the time and date). (cousin Shonda asks). Do you want me to bring anything, who's cooking? (Toya). Oh, nobody, you can bring some liquor! It's just a get together, nobody's cooking, I'll probably have some chips and dip(Shonda) What! Okay I'll let you know if I'm gonna come or not, I gotta check my schedule. (Toya) Okay let me know so I can get a head count. (Shonda) Okay, bye! (Shonda hangs up and says), shit, no fucking food, who the hell she think is coming, when there's no damn food. Bring alcohol, b***ch I need to eat! Shhh not me, (f bomb) out of here! (lmao). (smh black people). Chips and dip, what the (f bomb) I look like, I need food dammit! (sucks teeth) (ctfu). Let me call Tina and tell her this shit(lmao).

On the other hand, White people are more reserved. They will eat before they come and just drop off the gifts. They so nice (lol). It doesn't bother them as much as it bothers Black people. White people will just make a comment to their spouse, or girlfriends, how rude that White person was for not having refreshments but that the family wanted that gift. They don't make a big deal. White people know that, that is not all a party is about. Food is important.

The interviews I have conducted expresses how some Black and White people have grown with their families, and what foods made up their menus at home. How they cook and eat as an adult and how they have taken those traditions and implemented it in their everyday life with their families. This first interview is with a Black woman named Tiffany.

<u>Interview:</u>

Author: What kinds of food did you eat as a child?

Tiffany: My mom cooked a lot of meats. Pork chops, Steak, Meatloaf, Chicken. My Grandma would go into exotic foods like kibbie lubi, and Hungarian Goulash. My mom cooked all the time. Dad has his own place.

Author: Did your family eat at a dinner table?

Tiffany: Yes, we ate at the dinner table, especially for Sunday dinner. My gram would not let us skip it (lol).

Author: How was food prepared?

Tiffany: Food was prepared the day before for big holidays.

Author: What was your favorite food as a child?

Tiffany: I loved mom's baked chicken with crispy skin.

Author: As an adult now, do you eat a lot of the same foods you did as a kid? Is chicken still your favorite food?

Tiffany: Yes, it's a habit. But I expand and try new recipes. No, I'm a steak and potato kind of girl.

Author: Do you and your family eat at a dinner table?

Tiffany: We have been slacking because we are all occupied with work and activities.

Author: Do you practice some of your parent/parents traditions when cooking?

Tiffany: Yes, I have both gram and mom's recipes. But I use Pinterest a lot for my recipes. They are so good.

This second interview is with another Black woman who wished to stay anonymous:

<u>Interview:</u>
Author: What kinds of food did you eat as a child?
Anonymous Black Girl: My mom is Puerto Rican and Black, so we ate a lot of Spanish food. A lot of rice and peas.
Author: Did you help your mom or dad cook?
Anonymous Black Girl: I did help cook with my mother. I would stand on the chair and help her cook by age 6.
Author: Did your family eat at a dinner table?
Anonymous Black Girl: We ate at the dinner table sometimes. My mom was a single mom, so it was hard to get us all at the table.
Author: What was your favorite food as a child?
Anonymous Black Girl: My favorite food was Barbecue chicken. Actually, that's anything with barbecue sauce(lol). But my favorite of all is chicken & dumplings. I still ask her to make it.
Author: As an adult now, do you eat a lot of the same foods you did as a kid? Is chicken & dumplings still your favorite food?
Anonymous Black Girl: Yes, just about all the same foods.
Author: Do you and your family eat at the dinner table?
Anonymous Black Girl: When my kids were little, I tried to get them to eat at the table.
Author: How do you prepare food?
Anonymous Black Girl: I kind of took over for all holiday cooking.

Author: Do you practice some of your parent/parents' traditions when cooking?

Anonymous Black Girl: I can't cook a lot of the Spanish foods that she makes. I won't cook ham at all. Don't like it, and she(mom) cooks it(lol).

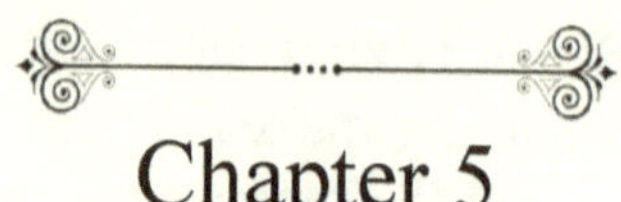

Chapter 5
Relationships

Relationships are built on trust, loyalty, love and honesty, whether it be with a family member, your kids or a companion, you should adhere to these concepts of a healthy relationship. Black and White people are different in how we pick friends, and who we choose to be in a relationship with. Some people are so racist that they can't see passed their own selfishness. Times have definitely changed on how we view relationships. At the end of this chapter, we will view some interviews from both parties on how they pick friends and who they would rather be in a relationship with. Today, we are dealing with a worldwide pandemic, that is questioning our community relationships. We are in this together, but some people still haven't changed their perspective on how important it is to come together as a nation. Racism will never end unless we as a people want it to.

Now, I did a little research on how Black people view relationships with either picking friends or picking individuals as a companion. A lot of these decisions come from how people are brought up from a child. When you get older, you decide how you want to live your life with the exception of taking in some family morals and teachings to one day pass on to your own children. Being a Black woman myself, I don't necessarily have a preference of how I pick friends. I grew up in the projects of Brooklyn, NY, so there were really no White people. It's predominantly Black, so naturally you would have Black friends. As I got older and went to different parts of NY, you see different people. Not until I moved to PA, did I encounter a predominantly White neighborhood. See in the Big Apple, majority of White people lived in the city part. On the out skirts and such. Some of my teachers were White, but we also had intelligent and smart Black teachers. In PA, you were bound to have contact with White people. I did not grow up prejudice, but you learn different things when you get older. You see how racist people are. I never cared if my friends were Black or White, because I wasn't taught to be racist. See it starts at home. I made friends with all kinds of people. I have White friends and Black friends. If you are true to me, then I am true to you. Only real friends stay with you forever. I had to learn the hard way when you consider your friends like family. Some relationships can't be fixed. "Some people are brought into your life for a reason, a season or a lifetime." Which is a famous poem from an unknown author, according to Google. Not everybody is meant to be in your life. I don't have a preference, because you can get Black girlfriends that will act like your friend, but then stab you in the back, because their jealous or miserable. But then you may get the White girlfriend that loves you to death and only wants the best for you. It's just the person. Not everyone has an agenda. I guess if we click like that and can vibe and talk about intelligent things without looking for a debate, then we can be friends. Only real friends will keep in touch, they hang out with you, your kids and they kids may play together. You and him/her can agree to disagree without a fight. I don't have a preference when it comes down to making relationships with people. Now being in a relationship is a little different, when picking a mate. Because I have always dated Black guys, I am not attracted to White guys. Don't get me wrong, there are some White men that I would love to take home, but there has not been any that has tried to holla (lol). I know how to flirt, but I have never actually walked up to a White guy and said, "Hey you wanna go out with me?"

No, I have not, so the chance has not come. For me White guys don't seem strong enough for me. Some seem very weak and I don't like guys that are clingy, because I like my space. Not that they are all like that. But I gravitate better to a Black guy. They don't have to be dark skinned, but Black. I like some kind aggression in my man. But not one that wants to fight me. But one that will beat a dude's ass for messing with his woman (lol). Now I just listed my preferences on how I pick men to be in a relationship with as a Black woman and person.

Now, I did a little research on who Black people are friends with and who they choose to be in a relationship with.

Judy Belk is a Black woman who is the president and CEO of the California Wellness Foundation. She wrote an article in June of 2020 about Interracial friendships, and how they can be "gratifying" but also "complicated". (Belk) In this article she states why she has the White friends that she does. She has a

Black husband, by choice, but she makes some valid statements. She has been plagued with racist remarks and racist situations but is still not racist. She states that she has a strong network of White friends who pass the test. She uses this test for anyone, no matter the color of their skin. She states, they are comfortable in their own skin, they can talk about race without gasping, they are loyal and committed. They have courage, is fun and interesting, and they don't ask to touch her hair (lol). (Belk). That's what I call a person that doesn't look at color as an issue.

Not that every Black or White person is racist, but the ones that are make the world more divided, because it affects the children of our future. They look up to us to make this world better for them.

White people on relationships and picking friends is a lot different. Most grow up in predominantly White privileged neighborhoods. They are rarely around other Black people. White people tend to associate themselves with people that are like them. People that identify with their lifestyle. This comes from going to all White schools where Blacks were not allowed. It is said that White people have less Black friends than Black people have White friends. Per CNN Breaking US & World News, an article from August of 2013, a Reuters poll showed that 40% of White people have zero non-White friends, and 20% of White Americans have 5 or more non-White friends (CNN). I do know from experience that White people don't know how to approach Black people. They say all the wrong things to try and make it seem like there not racist. Like when they say, "I have Black friends, how could I be racist." Well, why do you have those Black friends? What happened? I think that White people think that making friends with Black people so that they can still feel inferior is a problem. You're not physically saying that you don't like Black people, but your actions and how you handle a dire situation tells it all. There are articles circulating of individuals that have written about how their White friend from years turned their back on them after they didn't want to have the conversation about racism. I won't go into details, that's for another book, but once the subject comes about, the White friend doesn't want to talk about it. It should be talked about, to expand the mind on how the division of interracial friendships and relationships are affecting our society. It's a conversation that must be had. There was one article and I'll just briefly acknowledge the discrepancies where there was a longtime friendship with this Black and White woman. They were friends for years. When the "Black Lives Matter" movement came about, the White friend stated that "All Lives Matter," which sparked an underlying feud with her best friend who is Black. The Black woman wanted to have the conversation that it's because Black men are being killed by White police officers. The controversy is with Black people not all people. When the Black woman tried to make her friend understand, she simply stated that she didn't want to get involved and wouldn't answer her phone or return any phone calls. That resulted in the end of their friendship. Apparently, the friend was actually concerned with her own feelings about it and when her friend let her know that it wasn't about her, the conversation was over. We really need to do better people. According to the Daily Mail a 34-year-old White man wanted some tips on how to date a Black woman. His response was, he grew up in a Southern American State, he said he grew up in an area without Black people and had never spent time alone with someone of another race. He states he only knew about Black people from the news, stereotypes and moves. He's worked with Black people, but never really spoke to them, interesting. He does admit he is not a social person and knows nothing (Daily Mail).

I have conducted some interviews from both parties to give you a little insight on actual human responses: The first 2 interviews are with 2 Black women:

Interview:
Author: Do you have a preference when befriending people? (Making friends)
Tiffany: Yes, I like good people, and funny people. If you can make me laugh, that's a plus. Just honest and kind huma n beings.
Author: Would you say you have more Black friends or White friends?
Tiffany: It's a mix of both. I don't pick people off of skin color. I basically pick people off of their vibe.
Author: Do you have more guy friends or more girlfriends?
Tiffany: It's a mix of both. I have friends that I went to school with as a child that we are still friends. I have 3 guy friends. So, I guess more girlfriends.
Author: Say you and your White girlfriend go out and you guys are eating dinner and the waiter says a

racist remark to your friend, what would you do?
Tiffany: I would definitely call the waiter out on it. I have a mouth on me (lol).

<u>Interview:</u>
Author: Do you have a preference when befriending people? (Making friends)
Anonymous Black Girl: Honestly, I prefer Black girls. I have a lot of Black friends. I gravitate more to Black people than White people. I just have more in common with Black people.
Author: Would you say you have more Black friends or White friends?
Anonymous Black Girl: I have more Black friends than White friends. I grew up in a predominantly White area. Until I got older, we moved to a different area. I made a lot of Black friends.
Author: Do you have more guy friends or more girlfriends?
Anonymous Black Girl: Not that I'm older, I have more female friends. Now that I am in a more serious relationship, I have fewer male friends.
Author: Say you and your white girlfriend are out and you guys are eating dinner, and the waiter says a racist remark to your friend, what would you do?
Anonymous Black Girl: I would defend her, and let the waiter know he was wrong. It's wrong and not tolerated.

Now we are going to hear from two White women:

<u>Interview:</u>
Author: Do you have a preference when befriending

people? (Making friends)

Jessica H: I don't have a preference. I go based on a person's vibe.

Author: Would you say you have more White friends or Black friends? Why?

Jessica H: I have more Black friends. My mom's family is all mixed. My father's side is all White. My grandma and others were more racist, so I wanted to experience outside of my culture.

Author: Do you have more guy friends or more girlfriends? Why?

Jessica H: I have more guy friends. I feel like females are so catty. I feel like guy friends will keep it real even if they are not interested.

Author: Say you and your Black girlfriend go out and you guys are eating dinner, and the waiter says a racist remark towards your friend, what would you do?

Jessica H: I would definitely say something in her defense, and I will go to the manager.

Author: Do you have a preference when it comes to dating? Would you date a Black guy?

Jessica H: Yes and no. I rather Black guys. I tried dating a White guy, but it just didn't work. White guys seem to be more possessive, and they turn me off.

Interview:

Author: Do you have a preference when befriending people?

Crystal Hughes: No, I don't have a preference. All people have hearts, it doesn't matter what color you are.

Author: Would you say you have more White friends or Black friends? Why?

Crystal Hughes: I have more Black friends. I feel like Black people have more respect than White people. I get along better with Black people.

Author: Do you have more guy friends or more girlfriends?

Crystal Hughes: I have more male friends than female friends. Males don't have all the drama that females do.

Author: Say you and your Black girlfriend go out and you guys are eating dinner, and the waiter says a racist remark towards your friend, what would you do?

Crystal Hughes: I would ask to speak to the manager and pull them to the side and let them know that it's inappropriate to make remarks to try and slander a Black person.

Author: Do you have a preference when it comes to dating? Would you date a Black guy? Why?

Crystal Hughes: Yes, I only date Black guys, honestly, me as a White woman. I attract Black men more than White men.

That takes care of the interviews for this chapter. I have picked Black and White people that don't tolerate or like the division that imitates our world today. So as we wrap up this chapter, keep in mind some of the reasons why Black and White people are different. The way we are brought up and our families backgrounds have a lot to do with how we view relationships, how we make friends and who we want to be in a relationship with. It's amazing how even the White women had the same inclination of why I don't date White men. Not that I'm racist, but Black and White men are very different when being in a relationship as per Black and White women. The good thing is that these four women will not tolerate racism of no kind. With that being said, there are still people in the world that will stand up to the inequalities and disrespect that some of us bring to our country. I want to thank you guys for your respected answers, see you in the next chapter.

Chapter 6
Work

In the world of working class people, Black and White people are divided in the jobs that they actually qualify for. We are all smart and intelligent people that deserve to be successful. But in the world that we live in, it just doesn't happen that way.

A career is an occupation that you ensure, which brings opportunities for progression. It's a significant period in one's life where you strive for greatness to achieve your lifelong goals. In the world of Black and White people, we may strive for the same things, but because of inequalities that Black people are faced with, we don't get the same things. Granted you should have an exceptional education, but let's be real, all careers require us to be smart(lol).

A black person could have 5 degrees in different fields and struggle to find a job in that field. A White person could have less degrees and get multiple job offers from different companies. That doesn't add up. Black people are just as good at what they do. Black people fight every day to have a chance at success. What is happening is that we are starting to open up more and more of our own businesses, because of the lack of respect given for our achievements. Black people don't treat White people like they treat us. Hell, we are the ones that bust our asses to take care of them, because their own kind either tries to rob them, kill them or take advantage. It takes us to come in and protect White people, but we are the most hated and disrespected. Black people are always being told you don't have any experience, well that's why I need somebody to hire me, so I can get the experience I need to do the job. Especially when you have to go through training anyway(smh).

Black people are rarely recognized for their achievements and hard work. A White person will hire Black people because it looks good to hire minorities. It's actually against the law to discriminate, but it still happens. Prime example, I am a Black woman and I have 3 degrees, plenty of skills, and have been in healthcare for over 15 years. I have numerous jobs under my belt, but I am nowhere near where I would like to be. I have had good and bad jobs. A lot of the jobs I have had, have not lived up to my expectations. I am very smart and a fast learner. I live for helping and caring for people, mostly the elderly because they need us. One of my last jobs was working in a Group Home with intellectually disabled adults, which doing Home Health allowed me to already have had clients of this origin. I bust my ass every day to make sure that house was in tip top shape. I took the clients wherever they had to go, I did all the shopping. There was nothing I didn't do. My supervisor expressed to me that because of me being such a good worker they were going to make me a team lead for that particular house. The money was great, and I was finally going to be in control. For once I was going to move up fast. I deserved it, and then boom, this White lady comes along and destroys it. She was not a team player, she was already making rude comments about me to other coworkers that I didn't even know. Mostly everybody that came to work at that house, did no work. I didn't trip though, I just didn't talk to them, like they didn't talk to me. They would stay on their phone. There was maybe two or three people that I did talk to. This woman had every intention of trying to steal my job and my joy and I expressed that to my supervisor, and she would make it seem like I was bugging out. One day this woman got mad because I went to the store to get products because there was none left for the clients. I couldn't go before because there was not enough of us to stay with the clients, so I had to wait. When I was able to go I did, well she comes in while there's another staff member with me, which just so happened to be a lead from a different house, that I was actually cool with. She pulls me to the side and then proceeds to yell in my face(in aww). I kept my composure and let her know if she had a problem to speak to the supervisor. I immediately called my supervisor and let her know everything, and that I also had a witness. This lady was just out to get me for whatever reason. Not too many Black girls came to that house, maybe two others. My supervisor on many occasions always would tell me to calm down, and I constantly would tell her I am calm. White people always think a Black person is angry, which is another chapter we will cover. I was working through an agency, and I would tell my recruiter what they were doing to me. They wind up letting me go right before Independence Day and told my recruiter that they got a lot of complaints from my coworkers.

What bullshit, especially since they did nothing to that lady. They would constantly tell my recruiter how much of a good worker I was, and never mentioned coworkers complaining. Any situation that occurred there, I let my supervisor know and she didn't believe anything I said, but she believed her kind(smh). I was devastated of the news and suffered financially after that. I have to look at it like it wasn't meant for me to stay at that company, because who knows what else would have happened. They have the worst reviews. I think that they hire Black people just to say that they hire minorities and then they fire them for no reason at all. I have learned that some White people will find anything to degrade your reputation, well try to anyway. They think they are better than Black people but guess what, you're not. Black people are capable of making history, like we are still doing. Since then I have been trying to open my own Group Home. I can't open up the one I want but helping any group of people is fine by me. Remember that Black people were the one's busting our asses in those cotton fields. White people needed us without us they couldn't do half the things. Black owned businesses are on the rise, so watch out.

According to a study conducted by Christian E. Weller in December of 2019, he states that Black people have a higher unemployment rate than White people, why am I not surprised. It also states that Black people have lower pay and poorer benefits (Weller). Those differences are not new and is still a problem today. Black people also have the hardest time with securing a job fast enough. The Civil Rights Movement has made an impact on the systematic rights of Black people. There have been some improvements, but there is still work to be done. Black people experience so much racism, that it enables us to have the wealth of White people. Black people regardless of our education still deal with being overworked, underpaid, and racially profiled for our past and present indiscretions (smh).

Ex. I finally had gotten into the hospital of my choice, but the pay they offered was low for my qualifications and skills. They told me they couldn't budge for a higher rate (bullshit). I took it because I know that I am a great worker and will get my job done promptly and professionally. Well, we had two people leave around the same time, so they had to find new workers. They did they hired one girl, and then two more. Well guess what, they raised the pay rate, and they were making way more money than me. Even after they gave us a raise, they still made more than me to start and they weren't even there for the raise (smh). So unfair, and this is the reason why as a country we are still divided because of acts like this.

As a White person in the workforce, they tend to get the jobs they want. They rarely get told, "they are not a good fit." Some of them are the WORST employees ever. They think they are entitled, and always looking to getting someone in trouble instead of worrying about themselves. I noticed that the young White females, pick these jobs like healthcare, so that they can get paid, but they don't do them jobs. They are lazy and they don't put into perspective that people need to be taken care of properly. We would all love a paycheck but do your job. Some Black people are like that too, but White people don't get warned and fired faster than Black people. White people can have the same education and still get a better job. The problem is the innate way that White people control the workforce. There are numerous studies that focus on why this is a problem. Well, it's because of the racial segregation that still exists in the U.S. The labor market has concentrated a race to be under appreciated in society.

The more, White people that control the workforce, the more segregated and racist the world is going to stay. As I research and read why the segregation of employment is so against Black people being equal. It is a terrible thing that it's our justice system that allows this behavior. Mainly because it's ruled by the White man himself. Since the Jim Crow Laws, the purpose is still in effect. There are still places that practice the injustice of what it stands for. According to Anthony Carnevale a research professor at Georgetown University and Director of the University's Center on Education and the Workforce, who is also a co-author of the study, he states that we are a culture that keeps "secrets" from ourselves (Carnevale). He claims that even though workers increase their education, wage discrimination is reduced, but it still remains (Carnevale).

He also states that "you can get rid of discrimination, but this is a structural problem." (Carnevale). He is absolutely correct, hands down. The structure of our government is all wrong. It doesn't matter if you take all the White people out and put all Black people, that is not going to help. We as a nation need smart and intelligent people that's not going to tolerate racism, who is going to put an end to the injustices brought upon Black people and others. There has to be an uplift of congress and the laws that they allowed to discriminate against Black people for so many, many years. People have to be willing to do better.

White people continue to hold the better jobs. They continue to get the better education, even the ones that don't, hold better jobs and make more money.

I have conducted some interviews from previous clients, in regards, to how they make out with work and careers. There are two White women and two Black women. First, well hear from the two Black women.

Interview:
Author: What is your occupation?
Tiffany: Corporate Account Coordinator for food chains. Been at my job for 7 years.
Author: What is your passion? What do you like to do?
Tiffany: Business is my passion. I like that it changes every day. I like building relationships with corporate and the business chains. I like everything to run as smooth as possible.
Author: Are you doing what you love to do?
Tiffany: Yes, I do love my job. I get to grow and move up. I tried to go into the medical field, but it wasn't for me.
Author: What kind of jobs do you apply for? Do you ever get the jobs you actually want? Why or Why not?
Tiffany: When I was applying for jobs, I went with a

temp agency and landed my current employment. I have had less than 10 jobs in my life. I usually get any job that I have applied for thankfully. I did computer science, but it was boring. The medical field was too gory and when I got into the businesses field, I can tell the truth and it's recognized and accepted and applauded.

Author: What is the reason if any they went with someone else?

Tiffany: I have been let down from a promotion. The reason I was given was because I needed to grow more a s a business professional with the little, I held at that time. I needed more experience before I could advance forward. It was understandable, and that advice led me to the position I am in right now.

Good for you Tiffany, because not everyone is that lucky, keep up the good work!!!

The next interview is with our anonymous Black girl.

Interview:

Author: What is your occupation?

Anonymous Black Girl: Customer Service Representation, Front Desk Clerk.

Author: What is your passion? What do you like to do?

Anonymous Black Girl: When I was younger, I wanted to be a Fashion Designer. But I have been doing Customer Service for years and I'm good at it. I am thinking about going back to school for Criminal Justice.

Author: Are you doing what you love to do?

Anonymous Black Girl: No, but what I'm good at is, I love to advocate for everyone, especially women, Black women in particular.

Author: What kind of jobs do you apply for? Do you ever get the jobs you actually want? Why or Why not?

Anonymous Black Girl: Normally Customer Service. I do good in an office setting. Not always, but the jobs I have now I got right away. The Front Desk job is new for me.

Author: What is the reason if any do employers tell you is the reason, they went with someone else?

Anonymous Black Girl: Actually, last year, I applied for a job, it was a good interview, and everything, but then I got an email saying they were not hiring anymore. I was told, my interviewer said she didn't like me, and she just happened to be White.

Now we listen to answers from our White interviewees.

Interview:

Author: What is your occupation?

Jessica H: Manager at a Bar establishment

Author: What is your passion? What do you like to do?

Jessica H: I love the Hospitality Business. I have worked in Bars and Restaurants since age 16. I eventually want to open my own event planning business.

Author: Are you doing what you love to do?

Jessica H: Yes, I'm a people person. I want people to have a good time and enjoy themselves when they come to the Bar.

Author: What kind of jobs do you apply for? Do you ever get the jobs you actually want? Why or Why not?

Jessica H: It was always Bars and Restaurants. I tried Call Center jobs, but I don't like to be at a desk. I like to move around. Yes, for the most part. My experience allows me to get the positions.

Author: What is the reason if any do employers tell you is the reason, they went with someone else?

Jessica H: No, I have never had that happen before.

Lastly:

Interview:

Author: What is your occupation?

Crystal Hughes: I am a manager at a fast-food chain.

Author: What is your passion? What do you like to do?

Crystal Hughes: I would love to be a Crime Scene Investigator. I like to examine the bodies and find out who don't it.

Author: Are you doing what you love to do?

Crystal Hughes: Yes, because I'm a manager, it will open up more opportunities.

Author: What kind of jobs do you apply for? Do you ever get the jobs you actually want? Why or Why not?

Crystal Hughes: I apply for Warehouse, fast-food and working in a hospital or even Department Stores. Yes, I have always gotten the job I apply for.

Author: What is the reason if any do employers tell you is the reason, they went with someone else?

Crystal Hughes: This has never happened to me.

Thank you all for your responses. If you notice that for the last question for the two white women, they have never had an employer deny them of a position. But the two Black women have had that happen. Coincidence, I don't think so! Our work and careers should be based on our education and skills, leaning more towards skills, just because you may not have a Bachelors or a Masters Degree, doesn't mean that you are less capable of completing an assignment. Mostly all jobs require training.

Nowadays when completing an application for employment, there has been some added features, that require your truthful answers, like "are you a protected Veteran," or my time favorite, "What is your ethnicity," like it matters, BUT it does people! Even though employers give you that whole paragraph at the end of about being an equal opportunity company, which is bullshit, they still discriminate. I actually tried this out recently to see what my application would do. Well, I decided not to answer the million-dollar question of if I'm Black, White etc. I picked the "don't want to answer" bubble. Low and behold, it gave an error, the question must be answered. Why would you give that option if it's bogus? They want to know your race so they can pick and choose who to hire.

There was a randomized field experiment conducted by two researchers. They sent out thousands of resumes to sales, administrative and clerical jobs in the states of Boston and Chicago. They assigned either Black sounding or White sounding names. The resumes had a variety of different experiences.

These jobs were either going to call back or e-mail back for an interview. As I figured before reading this article, the White sounding names received 50% more call backs than those with Black sounding names(J-PAL). This is a clear indication of how screwed up and racist our world is. It goes to show, that we are not equal, there are still obstacles that we still have to face. We could never be the same. So, before you go saying "Oh we're all the same," smack yourself first and then go read a book, because that still does not indicate how racist you may be. You don't have a clue because you live in a White world.

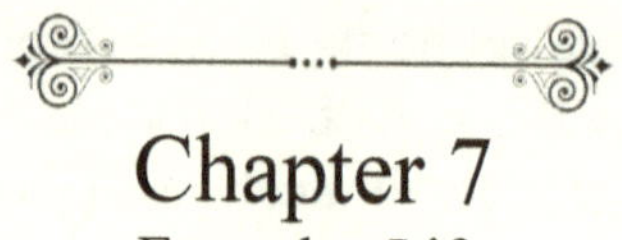

Chapter 7
Everyday Life

L ife as we know it is not at all easy, especially in these trying times of disparity. We try to cherish every moment with our loved ones, because tomorrow is not promised. We each as a culture live life differently every day. Black and White people live very different lives every day. This comes from how we were brought up and how we decide to live our lives once we leave the nest. The teachings that we take with us, should be held with the utmost respect and gratitude. As you grow into your human structure of what a human being should be, you evaluate how you want to start the next chapter of your life. You decide on the kind of husband or boyfriend you want. You ponder about the kind of career you're looking for and also how many kids you want to bare.

Well, when you think about it, you really have no control of that part(lol). God makes whatever possible, and he also doesn't give you as much as you can handle. I strongly believe that if he wants you to have a boy and a girl, then you're going to have that boy and girl. He knows the kind of person you are, and he also knows what you're going to do with what he gives you. You know how you hear somebody say, "God knew what he was doing when he gave me my one and only boy." Yes, he does because if he gave you anymore it wouldn't be right. Some people just have too many kids and can't even take care of them, but I think it's because he is teaching you a lesson of life. He wants you to figure out what you're doing wrong and fix it. I'm no psychic, but I listen and pay attention. I think it's my sixth sense. I can read people very well and can almost tell what they are thinking. I can almost sense a cry for help.

God gave me that! This chapter we're going to talk about our everyday lives that we live and how different they are. Let's explore some distinctive characteristics of how Black and White people live different lives. Shall we, we shall!

Black people live in a world where everything is Black and white. Every day for us is a survival tactic. We fight every day to stay alive. We fight every day to leave a mark in this world. I am somebody and we fight every day to prove that. Black people as we know live in a predominantly White society, where they see racism every day. Everything that is taught and learned, comes from White society. The Black excellence is ignored among the ignorance of the White man. I myself have endured many racial discriminatory acts, by many White people and it's always disputed with I'm overreacting.

White people are so bold, that they antagonize the Black race and then want to contact the authorities when you want to beat their racist ass! It's unfair, especially if you're defending yourself from the prejudices that align. If the shoe was on the other foot a Black person would be brutalized and shoved in jail, because of the color of our skin. Black people have to deal with police brutality. The authorities pick and aggravate Black people because of jealousy and prejudice. They think they can run the world and everything in it, because our government enhances those beliefs of misconduct and discrimination. The White dominance doesn't stop some of us from excelling. Black people are used to fighting, this is a way of life.

Everyday living for a Black person is dealing with racist store owners, racist employers and co-workers, getting healthcare rejections because of pre-existing conditions. Black people don't let it go, we speak up, we protest, we sometimes vandalize without understanding that it's our neighborhoods that we are vandalizing because we are mad. Not the best solution, but sometimes there's no way to send a message, unless you're violent. Guess what, it's the same way White people get our attention, by violence. They kill our people left and right and they don't apologize for it. None of the actions set forth by Black and White people help a situation. It makes it worse but can also make people way to communicate the injustices and let White people know that we are not having it anymore. We won't stand for it. We are and we will fight back!

White people on the other hand live carefree every day, without a care in the world. They can walk out their door every day and have no worries. They can get good health insurance they can go into a grocery store without the clerk or owner thinking you're stealing. They control every aspect of this world we call a nation. White people have "White privileges." They think they are entitled to everything. When you live a selfish and sheltered life of despair, those characteristics are upheld.

For the Black woman we live different than White woman. Take our hair. Black women get their hair done, we not getting in no water. Our DNA makes our strands very different from White women. White women can get their hair done and go swimming the next damn day (smh). We dress different. Black people dress more Urban, like name brand jeans, timbs, or a pair of Jordans. White people dress like White people (lol). Okay. Like uppity, like very professional all the time. They are always dressed so casual (lol). Their dress down, consists of slacks and a blouse. It's not all the time you see a White woman with jeans on. They tend to think they are under dressed if they wear things like that. Black and White people fight for different things every day. Never the same things of course.

There are very few White people that fight every day for social justice, for Black lives, for desegregation. Black people have to fight for themselves every day. So, before we say how we are not different, think about what Black and White people as a division, endure on an everyday basis. Think about what we face every day individually. Think about what you encounter on a day-to-day basis, and ask yourself, is it fair? Is this life?

Chapter 8
Learning

Black and White people learn different. We are taught things as kids, that we often take with us in our adult life. Whether what we learned was right or wrong, it was taught to us by our parents, grandparents, aunts, uncles and teachers. We decide as adults what we teach our own kids. <u>We decide what facts and fiction to teach them. We decide if we want to lead by example or follow like a crowd.</u>

Learning is a method of how we take in information. As humans we can learn from somebody telling us something, from somebody showing us, and learning hands on. Black and White people learn differently from one another. We are taught different things in life based on our culture, based on where we grew up, and based on who our parents are.

As a Black woman, I was taught a lot as a child. I went to a public school after I was enrolled in a private school, once we moved to Brownsville, Bklyn houses. I made a lot of friends quickly. We had the best teachers. Some were White and some Black. They taught us everything. We learned penmanship, which mines was always beautiful(lol). We learned computers, we learned science, we had projects, we also had music class. Art was amazing, as I was quite the little artist. We went on a lot of educational outings. My first time going to the White House was in 3rd grade. Our White teachers made sure we got everything out of learning without question. We also had a Muslim teacher, he was soo smart, he was our science teacher. Our math teacher was a scholar and boy, was he smart, I forgot but he was from a different country. He taught us math the way we understood. It wasn't a trick or difficult to learn. It was all for us. It was a predominantly Black school, but it was mixed, and everybody was treated the same. School was sooo much fun that none of us wanted to leave, so they made a middle school. They put in 2 more grades 7th, 8th and then we would go to HS.

Learning back then was important. We learned about famous Black and White people. My mother and grandmother didn't have to struggle to teach us much, when it came down to school. They were only responsible for teaching us etiquette and manners. I read a lot, so I was considered a "book worm," much like I am now(lol). I learned how to be strong from them. I'm a great cook by the way (lol). But overall school was our safe haven and our educational supplier.

When I was in H.S, we learned about different authors, and it still increased our minds of the world to come. We were the new millennium knowing about apartheid and racism was important. We had to read books like, "To Kill a Mockingbird," "The Diary of Ann Frank." We were taught about the holocaust. It wasn't a joke it was real events that affected the world at some point. The curriculum back then meant something. These were material information that we would definitely need as adults and some to teach our children if all else fails.

Nowadays, I don't know what the hell these teachers think they are teaching. The school system NOW is ridiculous. These kids don't learn anything valuable. They don't learn penmanship; they don't learn about their Black culture. The only famous Black person they learn about is Dr. Martin Luther King Jr. What happened to everybody else. Too controversial that the kids can't read how racist White people were back then and still are now. The things they learn now is irrelevant to society, and it's not taught correctly. I can't even help my youngest daughter who is in the 7th grade now with her Math. The teachers teach them the most difficult way, that I don't think the smartest person in the world could understand. So, I have to tell her to do it how her teacher showed her, so that I don't confuse her. I don't even understand it (smh). What is going on, but yet you don't see anybody fighting the school systems to change the curriculum. It's like they want to see these kids fail. They are so worried about money and power and trying to beat China, that it's only hurting our children.

Being out of school during this Covid-19 pandemic is making a lot of the students stupid. They can't get a good education online. Some kids can't learn that way. Technology is not all it's cracked up to be. These kids are always put into categories to determine how smart they are, or how smart they should be. Black history should not be celebrated 1 month out of the year, it should be celebrated everyday like White predecessors. So, when I mean how Black people learn and what they are taught, I mean just that. All

Black people are not wholesome or are willing to forgive and forget. Some are more racist than some White people. I think the reason for that is they are angry and blaming all White people, which is a little absurd especially when there's White people that are on our side. The anger has to be directed to the source, and the present problem makers.

I particularly teach my kids morals and other people's behaviors because I have been around longer, and I have learned a lot from people and reading. I don't sugar coat shit; I am very raw. I correct certain things that they learn. I teach them about life and all the things that could go wrong. But most importantly I let them be them. They are all 3 different so I expect different things. Life is what you make it. I encourage them to read a lot and learn things on their own instead of asking me all the time (lol). I don't know everything.

Now when talking about how White people learn is a lot different. They are also brought up in a predominantly White neighborhood and are taught their culture. But because they seem to think they rule the universe, like God gave them that title, they tend to uphold the "White Privilege" analogy. They learn the racist remarks from their parents, grandparents, teachers etc. Their parents were taught how to be racist, and it passes down from generation to generation. Don't get me wrong, not every White person is racist, but it's not hard to find the ones that are.

Ex. I read an article about a Black teacher that was teaching his class and one of his 10yr old students which was White asked if he was afraid as a Black man to get shot and killed by a police officer (wow). The teacher of course was astonished and surprised that this child even thought to ask that question. He didn't really know how to answer, but he was grateful to the student for wanting him to answer. He wanted to be honest, because the student deserved the truth. After giving his truth, more and more students started asking questions. So, there it was, an introduction to the topic of racism. The next day his principal approached him because a White parent complained about the discussion, that was brought about from one of his White students. The principal explained to him that the White parent commented "I don't understand why he would be afraid of the police unless he is doing something illegal." The principal gave his full support on discussing racism with his students (Gillard). How disgusting is that. White people have no idea what it's like to be Black and they never will. They just don't get it. So, when I mean that White people learn and how they are taught, I mean just that. White parents have a lot to do with how their kids are taught. They seem to think racism is not real. And again, we learn from our parents, grandparents, and teachers.

In another article by Ali Michael and Eleonora Bartoli, Ali discusses how growing up in a suburban Midwest part of the world, he never talked about racism with his family. There was a neighborhood of only White people. There was never a reason to talk about it. But later in life he realized that he was blind to the fact when trying to talk about something you don't know. He then realized that this came from not being taught this as a child. Interesting, but not surprising. White people have a tendency to not talk about what they don't think has happened or is happening. They don't think anything is wrong. There are plenty of articles for White people to read, listen and understand. There is nothing wrong with not being taught it at an early age but being ignorant to the fact in later years is a problem. I understand if your parents didn't want to tell the truth, but it's up to you as an adult to learn about the discretions that divide this country. It's racism at it's all time high. Times have definitely gotten much worse.

White people, we must do better, in teaching and learning about the world around us. These differences are real and won't stop unless everybody is on board. It's not all White people, but the vast majority of them need a lesson or two on humanity.

Chapter 9
Parenting

A parent is someone that takes care of their offspring (children). They are there to cloth them, feed them, bathe them and teach them right from wrong. I have been a parent for the last 20 years. It is a wonderful feeling, to wake up to your children every day. Don't get me wrong it can be hard as your child/children get older, but it's well worth it. I have 3 girls, my oldest is 22, my middle daughter will be turning 17 soon, and my baby is 14. They will always be my babies. They are the light of my life, and I would do anything for them, just like my mom does for her four girls. Anybody can make kids but being there and actually taking care of their every need, makes you a parent. You can grow up in a two-parent household or a single parent household, nobody is perfect (lol).

Black and White people parent soooo different, I almost couldn't wait to get to this chapter to kick some knowledge to those people that don't know how to parent, or to the one's that think they are the greatest parent, but they don't have a clue. I know that everyone thinks they are the best parent ever, and you should. But there is always room for growth, some too late. There are no books that tell you what to do in case you come across a difficult situation with your kids. A lot of information is learned from a young age and then you put your own spin on it that then fits your lifestyle. Nobody shouldn't be telling you as a parent, how to parent, but there are always times when you could use some advice. Opinions shouldn't be accepted because everybody parents differently and each kid is different. There are definitely things that shouldn't be tolerated like disrespect, cursing, yelling etc. from a child, but that doesn't stop some kids. I don't know how some parents tolerate that kind of behavior. My kids would be six feet under if they did any of that nonsense (lol). Kids learn this behavior from their parents, and from their friends. If you get kids in order at an early age, and not think everything is funny, half of them would not end up the way they do. Now I know that we can't control everything about our kids, when they reach a certain age, but as a child they should not have any of those tendencies. If the discipline is in place, then a lot of situations that arise with some children wouldn't happen. Grant it we can't stop them from a lot of the dangers of the world, because peer pressure is serious and because the generations are sooo different. We have a heavy flow of drugs, depression and anxiety that plagues our youth, we can't stop it all!

When children grow up, they do what they want to do. They want to experience life how they see fit, regardless of how they were brought up and also what we taught them. They want to try things because they want to. Addiction is very real. It has and still is killing our youth. I interviewed some parents to get a little information on their parenting. We will see their answers at the end of this chapter.

Black people's parenting is not easy. We have to have these tough conversations about racism and why certain things are tolerated. For Black people, we are constantly trying to protect our children. We have to protect them from people that's supposed to have their back like teachers, administrators and so-called friends (SELF). An article by Rozalyn S. Frazier c.p.t from SELF.com spoke with a variety of Black parents raising Black children on what parenting looks like right now in the 21st century. One parent stated that she tries to keep her child's innocence as long as she can, but every time you see the news there's always a reason to have the talk about racism (SELF). Another parent has a young son and she had to let him know what to do if they ever got stopped by the police. For her it's very hard because she has to instill in him that they will harm him. It's not television or a movie, it's real life. We never want to have to tell our son's this, but in all reality it's the truth.

I am a Black mother of girls no boys, but I teach them that they can do whatever they put their minds too. There is no limit. They understand that the world is not easy, and that certain people are going to try and shoot you down because of the color of your skin. They have not experienced racism, but they know what to do if it should occur. They are not disrespectful, and they know to tell me, or their dad and we will take care of it. This is not all parenting is about. My girls are very smart and independent. They don't get beatings because they don't do anything that terrible. They each have chores every day and it is to be followed, or I act like a crazy person. I will put them on punishment quickly where they can't go outside, or I take things away. My oldest daughter is 22 now, so she so doesn't get punished, but I will yell and threaten her and even not speak to her. She hates when I don't talk to her. All they know is mommy. Their dad is in the picture, well, my two oldest father is anyway. My 16yr old, which is the middle child can't sit still. She is very social and is always at her millions of friend houses. It's the same people all the time, so I'm fine with that. We know where she is at all times, and we know the parents. With her I have to punish her and the way to do that is make her ass stay in the house. It kills her (lol), job done. She actually is on punishment right now because we are in the middle of a pandemic so there is online school and she finds it hard, but she is not living up to her full potential and instead of asking for help she stays quiet. She is not doing her best and I play no games when it comes to education. She does what I did as a kid, walk around pouting like the world is going to end because she can't go outside(lol). That's her punishment, and she actually is on punishment more than her sister. My youngest daughter is 14. Her dad is not in the picture, because he's just a donor (lol). He is a crappy parent that doesn't have the drive to be a real parent. Anyway, she always has me. She is a big gamer. She plays video games every day after school. Now her punishment is to get off the game, no t.v. That hurts her because that's her world. But punishment is punishment. Now if I had to beat them I would. Nowadays, it's forbidden, but I personally defy that because a lot of these kids need their ass beat, because they are disrespectful and rude as hell. Black people don't tolerate that kind of behavior. If I had ever acted like some of these kids now, I wouldn't have no damn teeth. Where is the discipline. Most Black people don't have that issue, because we would definitely break our foot off in somebody's ass. Our Black parents didn't play that shit. My kids no better. They hate when I yell, they act right. I don't have that problem, because I raised them right. They are definitely spoiled because they don't want for nothing. But they know I would break their face if they ever lost sight of their manners.

Growing up my mother didn't play that. She would beat your ass. Discipline was a big thing. I got punished a lot because I didn't listen. I also didn't like to not be able to go outside. I learned my lesson though. As a teenager, I started to help take care of my little sisters. I was the oldest and my mother was a single parent in the household. She worked every day, so I took the liberty to take care of the household. I made sure my sisters did their homework, took baths, I did laundry, and cooked dinner. It was a routine to help my mother have little to do when she came home from work. I was always dependable and understood the struggle. She taught me well. That's what a parent is supposed to do. To teach you responsibility and mannerism.

Black parents don't play when it comes down to discipline. They will smack the taste out your mouth. Regardless, what anybody says. Nowadays it is said that you can't hit your kids. I don't know who made that up, but this is the reason these kids are out of control. Parents are scared to do anything to their kids because they could possibly go to jail. Not that you're trying to kill them but getting a beating shouldn't land you in jail. Because kids know that you can't put your hands on them, they call the police themselves. This is unacceptable because back in the day, you could beat a kid ass (lol). The world has changed so much. I don't know who came up with this updated show of discipline, but it is the worst concept of discipline.

I have seen White people parent and it's very unusual. I have White friends and some of their kids are out of control. They don't yell at them, they don't take things away, and they let them do whatever they want. Their kids have tantrums (smh). What is a damn tantrum anyway? They need their ass beat and that will straighten them out. I see White parents with their kids in supermarkets and Department stores, cursing at their mother. I watch the mother do nothing. They act like their scared (smh). I don't see how that's parenting. Your child is not supposed to curse you out and tell you what to do. Who birthed who? Then you got the White parents saying, "I give my child privacy, I don't go through their stuff, I don't go in their room unless I knock." Give me a damn break. This is why the kids are like that. I never heard that before. CHILDREN SHOULD NOT HAVE PRIVACY! I really want to know who taught White people how to parent. How do you let a child that came out of your body, curse you out, or even put they hands on you, that's insane? I have had White people ask me; how did you get your kids to behave like that? How are they supposed to behave? They are not animals. They know better. Some White people don't teach their children about racism. The one's that do, they teach them to be racist. It starts at home. Kids learn from the people they are around the most.

Some kids even know that it's wrong, but because their parent/parents make them do hideous things, they have to follow. White people also have this thing called time-out (wth). You see them pointing and counting. That doesn't do anything but piss the kid off and make them scream their heads off(lol). My time-out as a kid was go get the damn belt (lol). We must do better White people. I'm not saying to kill your children but be that force that they need to succeed in life. Be that parent that's not scared of their child. You hold the power not them. I get it some kids you want to choke them because their soo bad, but their bad because of us. Discipline goes a long way. Research shows how few White people actually have the talk of racism with their kids. Research also shows that White parents downplay the significance of racism in America. They state how we are all the same and there's no difference in race (The Conversation). White people you are putting your kids in a big bubble that doesn't exist. Racism is very real and should be talked about amongst family and friends. Nobody should be ignorant to the fact especially since this is an ongoing issue. White people you must do better!!!

Now I will share the answers to the interviews conducted. We are going to hear from a Black woman and a Black man. Well hear from the Black woman named Melissa R. first:

Interview:
Author: How were you brought up, in a single parent household or both parents?
Melissa R: I was brought up with 2 parents, but my

mom passed away when I was 4 yrs old. My dad raised me and remarried, and I had a stepmother the rest of my time. So, I always had both parents.

Author: Did you get beatings when you were a kid? What were your punishments as a child?

Melissa R: Yes, I got beatings, I got restricted from doing activities and no allowances.

Author: Do you have children? Do you punish them when they are misbehaving?

Melissa R: Yes, I have 2, 1 boy, 1 girl. Yes, but because they are older, I just strip them of their favorite things. They did get beatings as young kids, if needed.

Author: Would you say you're a strict parent?

Melissa R: No, not exactly because we were always on the go. I addressed things as needed. If I saw them doing something that was not right and repetitive, I would address it.

Author: At what age if any would you say your daughter or son can start dating?

Melissa R: My daughter, I am not thinking about dating at all. My son had little dates and stuff but not left alone. I would say about 16 and supervised.

Author: Would you rather a public school or private school for your child/children?

Melissa R: Private schools, I like the smaller environment it helps kids retain information. It's a very private environment. I like public schools because of the diversity kids need that. There are all nationalities for them to relate to.

Author: Are you religious? Yes, or no? Would you make your kids go to church? Why?

Melissa R: No, I don't go to church. I would not

make my children go, but I do want them to believe in something.

Author: What do you teach your kids about racism? What will you teach your child about racism? What were you taught as a child about racism?

Melissa R: For me, I try to show them their history. I make them watch important movies or shows to know the importance of racism whether videos, readings or etc.

Author: Do you give your kid/kids privacy?

Melissa R: No, they can't lock their doors. I have restricted social media. They cannot have freedom to do whatever they want.

Author: Did you or would you make your kid/kids go to college?

Melissa R: My kids are still young, but I will encourage them to pursue a goal. Not necessary college but to educate themselves on that goal to be successful.

The second interview is with a Black father who calls himself Mr. Brown Water.

<u>Interview</u>:

Author: How were you brought up, in a single parent household or both parents?

Mr. Brown Water: In a single parent house with my mother.

Author: Did you get beatings when you were a kid? What were your punishments as a child?

Mr. Brown Water: hell yeah, you should ask me when I didn't get a beating (lol). I got a beating and couldn't go outside. I would have to stay in my room.

I could only come out to eat and go to school.

Author: Do you have children? Do you punish them when they are misbehaving?

Mr. Brown Water: Yes, I have 2 daughters, and a stepdaughter. No, they do whatever the hell they want (lol). No, but they don't really do anything to get punished. I yell more than anything. I try to but they mother always trying to stop me, saying I'm mean.

Author: Would you say you're a strict parent?

Mr. Brown Water: I'm not strict, just with certain things.

Author: At what age if any would you say your daughter or son can start dating?

Mr. Brown Water: Never, (lol), I would say about 17, 18 yrs old. I want to meet them first.

Author: Would you rather a public school or private school for your child/children?

Mr. Brown Water: I don't have a preference. As long as they are learning what their supposed to learn.

Author: Are you religious? Yes, or no? Would you make your kids go to church? Why?

Mr. Brown Water: No, I wouldn't make them, but if they wanted to go, I wouldn't stop them.

Author: What do you teach your kids about racism? What will you teach your child about racism? What were you taught as a child about racism?

Mr. Brown Water: I would teach them that White people are no better than us, and we are no better than them. We are all equal, just a different color.

Author: Do you give your kid/kids privacy?

Mr. Brown Water: My oldest gets privacy with her phone. They get privacy in the bathroom. They can't lock their doors, but they can close them if they need to because their girls.

Author: Did you or would you make your kid/kids go to college?

Mr. Brown Water: I wouldn't make them go, but I would encourage them to go. College is not for everybody.

Thank you, Melissa R. and Mr. Brown Water for your interviews, your answers were greatly appreciated.

In talking about parenting, there is a big thing about when kids should date. I like the answers that these two Black parents one being a woman and the other a man. Young children especially teenagers shouldn't be worried about dating, they should be worried about school. Time and time again I see these little girls talking about their boyfriends, or young boys talking about their girlfriends. They are too young. My daughters are not allowed. I have a 16yr old, I wish she would tell me she has a boyfriend. My 22yr old is not dating at the moment, she had a boyfriend and now she is focused on herself, thank you Jesus(lol). You must protect your children at any cost. It is so many young White girls pregnant. I'm not saying little Black girls don't get pregnant, but the numbers don't match. As parents we need to be smarter. YOUR KIDS ARE NOT YOUR FRIENDS! We are parents at the end of the day. Kids having kids is terrible, because the parents are the ones who will have to take care of those babies.

I have friends that allow their young girls or young boys to have mates and spend the night at their homes. What in the mother fuck is wrong with you?

I know as a mother of girls, that they don't tell us everything, if you keep giving them so much freedom, they are going to run wild. We as parents and as human beings apart of a disorganized world must do better. It's okay if your kids say they hate you, they will get over it and in time will appreciate your pattern of discipline. We would have less uneducated and angry kids, if we showed more affection and attention.

P.S. Kids like when we as their parents and as adults tell them the truth. Stop lying to your kids, you make matters worse.

Chapter 10
Color

The color of our skin has always and will always be a revelation. There is Black and White. The two colors being different. They can never mean the same thing, and the only comparison is we are all human beings. The color of our skin makes everything different, how we are treated as a person, the schools we get into, the jobs we get, the loans we get approved for, and how we live as a person makes up the color of our skin, respectfully. See Black and White people live differently because of the color of our skin. The color of our skin defines a lot. It defines who we are as a whole and where we are going as a nation. We are not the same at all because of this. We look different for a reason. So, when people say they don't see color, it's a lie, you have to notice the inequalities because of the color of our skin. You must know that the social injustice in this world is because we look different. You could be a different ethnic group, but Black and White is always up for discussion.

In hopes that the new president and his team can try and minimize or get rid of racism, starting with Congress first, then maybe we can try to resolve the hatred that White people have for Black people. Maybe we can be a unified country because clearly, we suck at it!

Then there's the ignorant rant from White people, how Black people all look alike, which is bullshit, we are all Black but possess different features. It's the stereotypical quote that White people think it's not racist. News flash it is racist. Some people look alike but we as Black people don't mistake White people as all looking alike, but we could because some of you do.

Because of having our 45th president make racism even worse with his prejudices and lying to protect it. White people would like to believe that he was helping, but you have to realize who he was helping and it wasn't Black people. Racism is not new, but it has been on an all-time high since 2016. The amount of police brutality, and mistaken identities that have plagued this country in the last 4 years has been unbelievably disgusting. Our justice system and Congress should be ashamed, how they mocked civilization and all the historical fights that had to happen in order to try and shape this nation. The injustices are at an all-time high. It's going to take the new president and his team of newcomers to honor what our civil rights leaders have set in place for Black people and mankind.

FYI: Just remember who was fucking who back in the days to make our kids look different. White men couldn't keep their hands and their privates out the Black Forest.

Black people we are loved, Black people we are important, Black people we are strong, Black people we will WIN!!!

The End

References

1. Lynch, Hollis African Americans/ History & Culture/Britannica retrieved from Britannica.com

2. Drewry, Henry African American History/ Scholastic retrieved from
www.scholastic.com

3. www.history.com>topics>black-history>slavery

4. www.crf.usa.org>black-history-month>black-history Black History Month-Constitutional Rights Foundation

5. www.dictionary.com

6. April 9, 2019-www.pewsocialtrends.org views of racial inequality in America/pew Research Center

7. Civil Rights Movement: Timeline, key Events and leaders…… retrieved from
www.history.com>topics>black-history>civi-rights-M……

8. RACE-The Power of an Illusion/White Advantage retrieved from newsreel.org>guides>race>white adv

9. Brando Simeo Starkey March 1, 2017 Why do so many white people deny the existence of white retrieved from
theundefeated.com>features>why>do-so-many-white

10. Judy Belk 06/27/2020 Los Angeles Times Op-Ed: Interracial friendships can be complicated- Los Angeles Times

11. Aug 19, 2013 CNN.com Opinion -Why don't Whites have Black friends?-CNN-CNN.com

12. Sept 24, 2020-White man who took a black woman on a date, is flooded with advice on....retrieved from Daily Mail>uk>article
13. Christian E. Weller December 5, 2019 African Americans Face Systematic Obstacles to Getting Good Jobs retrieved from Center for American Progress
14. Elin Johnson October 18, 2019 Racial inequality, at college and in the workplace retrieved from IHE- Inside Higher Ed
15. Discrimination in the Job Market in The United States/ The Abdul Latif Jameel Poverty Action Lab>evaluation>d
16. Malcolm J. Gillard July 7, 2020 Do White People get it? Racism through the Eyes of a Black Male Teacher retrieved from Ed Week.org>
17. Ali Michael and Eleonora Bartoli 2014/2020/07/ What White Children Need to Know About Race- NAIS retrieved from https://www.nais.org>summer-
18. Rozalynn S. Frazier Oct 22, 2020 12 Black Parents of Black Children on Raising Their Kids Right Now/SELF
19. June 25, 2020 Most White Parents don't talk about racism with their kids- The Conversation

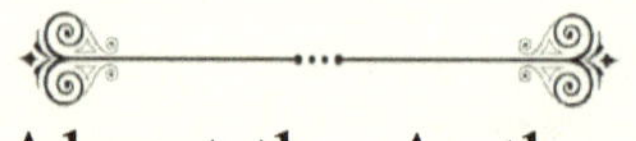

About the Author

My name is Latoya Williams, my friends call me Tee for short, and I am from Brownsville, Brooklyn, New York. I am a 43-year-old black woman who is the oldest of 4 girls, and I currently reside in Pennsylvania. I have 3 beautiful girls of my own, that I raise every day. I am a Service Coordinator with a healthcare entity based here in Pennsylvania. I have been in healthcare for over 17 years and proud of the care that I give every day. I used to write short stories as a little girl, but my passion has been to always help and care for people. My goal in life is to just continue to be me and not forget where I came from.